TALES OF OLYMPUS
A Greek Myth Musical

Book, Music and Lyrics by Min Kahng

YOUNG PERFORMERS VERSION

LICENSING & PRODUCTION INQUIRIES
Uproar Theatrics, LLC.
hello@uproartheatrics.com | www.UproarTheatrics.com

Setting:

Jason's bedroom and the main hall of Mount Olympus.

Character List (in Order of Appearance):

JASON – a young, socially awkward boy, 12

CALLIOPE – The goddess of epic poetry

HERMES – The messenger god

APHRODITE – The goddess of love and beauty

ATHENA – The goddess of wisdom (among other things)

ZEUS – The king of the gods

CRONOS – Greedy father of Zeus

RHEA – Caring mother of Zeus

HERA – The goddess queen

POSEIDON – The god of the sea

DEMETER – The goddess of the harvest

HESTIA – The goddess of the flame

HADES – The god of the Underworld

ARACHNE – A mortal weaver

ARACHNE'S ADMIRERS

MUSES (CLIO, URANIA, THALIA, TERPSICHORE, ERATO, POLYHYMNIA, EUTERPE, MELPOMENE)

ICARUS – A foolish son

DAEDALUS – Icarus' hard-working father

DESTRUCTION – self-explanatory

DISEASE – self-explanatory

HOPE – small but strong

PELIAS – Jason's uncle

AESON – Jason's father

ALCIMEDE – Jason's mother

CHIRON –A centaur, Jason's adoptive father

ORACLE – Blind, but sees all

HERACLES – He's so strong

ATALANTA – She fights like a lion

SIX-ARMED GIANT – self-explanatory

HARPIES – Hungry bird-women that want to eat everything in sight

AETES – King of Colchis

MEDEA – Sorceress daughter of Aetes

DRAGON – that never sleeps

Tales of Olympus: A Greek Myth Musical was originally commissioned and produced by Bay Area Children's Theatre.

Playwright's Note: An asterisk appearing next to a name indicates simultaneous singing or speaking with another character.

**For a 6-person adult cast version intended for school tours, please visit Uproar Theatrics

MUSICAL NUMBERS

#1.Opening: Intro – Instrumental

#2.He'll Tell Our Stories – CALLIOPE, HERMES

#3. Hermes' Message – HERMES

#4a-e. Olympus – ALL

#5a-b.The Baby Swallowing Song – ZEUS, CRONUS, RHEA, HERA, POSEIDON, DEMETER, HESTIA, HADES, GODS

#6a-d.I Used to Weave – ATHENA, ARACHNE, ARACHNE'S ADMIRERS, GODS

#7.Icarus & Daedalus – MUSES, ATHENA, ICARUS, DAEDALUS, GODS

#8.Aphrodite's Song – APHRODITE

#9a-c.Don't Open the Box – JASON, GODS

#10. Hope's Solo – HOPE

#11.Olympus (Reprise) – ALL

#12a-r.Be A Hero – JASON, CHIRON, HERA, PELIAS, HERACLES, ATALANTA, MEDEA, ZEUS, APHRODITE, DRAGON, GODS

#13a-c.Finale – JASON, GODS

#14.Bows – Instrumental

<u>**SCENE 1**</u>

> *(JASON'S bedroom. There is a bed, a bookshelf cluttered with sci-fi books and paraphernalia, and a window. JASON is asleep in bed.)*
>
> *(CALLIOPE, the goddess of epic poetry, appears at the window and peers in. She enters the room thru the window. She stands, looks at JASON and emits an excited gasp.)*
>
> *(She walks over to the sleeping boy.)*
>
> *(HERMES starts to enter from the window as well.)*

CALLIOPE

Hermes!

HERMES

I'm coming…

CALLIOPE

Ta-da!

HERMES
(excited at first, and then…)

What?

CALLIOPE

The boy!

CALLIOPE
HE'LL TELL OUR STORIES!
AND HE'LL MAKE US FAMOUS ONCE AGAIN

HERMES
TELL OUR STORIES?

CALLIOPE
Mm-hmm!

HERMES
(looking around the room)
Computer games? Science fiction novels?
    (coughs)
NERD!

CALLIOPE
He is not a nerd, Hermes! He's the next bard for the Greek
gods!

HERMES
Really?

CALLIOPE
Really! He's the one! Now, wake him up!

HERMES
Why do I have to wake him up?

CALLIOPE
Because you're the messenger god!

HERMES

And you're not my boss!

CALLIOPE

Hermes, we don't have time for this…

(HERMES relents.)

HERMES
(clears his throat)
HUMAN CHILD
I BRING A MESSAGE FROM THE GODS

(JASON snores loudly.)

HERMES

I gotta have Orpheus write me a new song.

CALLIOPE
(in JASON'S face)
WAKE UUUUUUP!!!

(JASON falls out of his bed, then suddenly stands upright, still in a haze.)

JASON

You will never defeat the intergalactic army, alien swine!
(waking up)
Huh? Where am I?
(sees CALLIOPE and HERMES waving)
AGGGH!!!! Strangers! Help! Help!

CALLIOPE

It's OK! It's OK! Sh!
> *(JASON stops and listens.)*

CALLIOPE

We just came to take you to our mountain.

JASON

AAGGGH!!!

> *(JASON trips and falls over the mess in his room.)*

HERMES

He's very coordinated, I see.

CALLIOPE

Oh, stop it.

JASON

> *(rises again)*

HELP!

> *(CALLIOPE waves her hand and JASON can no longer open his mouth.)*

CALLIOPE

> *(motions for him to have a seat)*

Jason, I am Calliope. Goddess of epic poetry. I usually inspire humans to speak, but in this case I had to do the opposite. Now, I promise we're not going to hurt you. If I let you talk again, do you promise not to run away?

> *(JASON gives a slow nod of his head.)*

CALLIOPE

Wonderful!
> *(waves her hand)*

See? We're just a couple of Greek gods in your bedroom. Nothing weird!

JASON

What do you want?

CALLIOPE

I'd like to take you to meet Zeus.

JASON

> *(overpronouncing it)*

Zoos?

CALLIOPE

Yup! He's our king.

JASON

King?

HERMES

That's right, kid. King of the gods! Get on his bad side and he'll ZAP you with his lightning bolts! POW! WAM!

CALLIOPE

Stop scaring him!

JASON

Why do you want me to meet him?

CALLIOPE

> *(with gravity)*

Because you could be our only hope!

CALLIOPE
ONCE WE WERE TOTALLY FAMOUS
FAMOUS AS FAMOUS COULD BE
EVERYONE KNEW WHAT MY NAME WAS
ALL THROUGHOUT ANCIENT GREECE
ONCE WE WERE LOVED AND RESPECTED
FEARED LEST OUR ANGER WOULD STRIKE
OH YOU SHOULDA SEEN
WHAT LIVING WAS LIKE

ON OLYMPUS

JASON
Olympus?

CALLIOPE
MOUNT OLYMPUS! THAT'S WHERE WE'RE FROM
OLYMPUS, THE MOUNTAIN OF THE GODS

JASON
I've never heard of Mount Olympus.

CALLIOPE
That's the problem!
> *(to HERMES)*
Help me, Hermes!

HERMES
WE WERE THE INSPIRATION
OF MANY STORIES AND MYTHS

CALLIOPE
POETS SANG OUR ADORATIONS
WE WERE THE FIRST "GREATEST HITS"

HERMES, CALLIOPE
FAST-FORWARD TO THE TWO-THOUSANDS
NOBODY KNOWS WHO WE ARE
SO WE'RE ON A SEARCH
TO FIND A NEW BARD

HERMES
FOR OLYMPUS, THAT SUMMIT ON HIGH

CALLIOPE
OLYMPUS, OUR HOME IN THE SKY

HERMES, CALLIOPE
OLYMPUS IS SEARCHING FOR A BARD

JASON
What's a bard?

CALLIOPE
Simply put, a bard is an epic storyteller!

JASON
There's no one like that here.

HERMES
Even the kid agrees…

CALLIOPE
Jason, *you* will be our next bard!

JASON

What?!

OH NO, YOU MUST BE WRONG
I'M NOT THE ONE YOU'RE LOOKING FOR
I'M NEITHER SMART NOR STRONG
MY ARMS ARE WEAK, MY GRADES ARE POOR
CALLIOPE, I'M FLATTERED JUST TO BE
CONSIDERED, MA'AM
BUT I CAN TELL YOU NOW I'M NOT THE GUY
YOU THINK I AM!

CALLIOPE

Jason…

JASON

AND
I CAN'T SPEAK PUBLICLY IN POEM,
LET ALONE IN WORDS
CAUSE WHEN I'M NERVOUS I START
SQUAWKING
LIKE A SICKLY BIRD
I'M NOT A SUPERSTAR OR GENIUS,
JUST LITTLE ME
THE BOY WHO LIKES TO READ HIS SCIENCE
FICTION/FANTASY!

HERMES

(coughs)

NERD!

CALLIOPE

Hermes! You're not helping!

JASON

No, he's right! I am a nerd! I've been diagnosed by the doctors as socially awkward! And I'm lactose intolerant!

HERMES
(walks toward the window)
We don't need to waste our time then!

CALLIOPE

Stop! Jason. You have the soul of a bard!

JASON

I do?

CALLIOPE

And you love stories! Those are two of the three most important bard requirements!

JASON

And the third one?

CALLIOPE

Bards should love telling stories!

HERMES
(messing with JASON)
In public.

JASON

I can't…

CALLIOPE

Jason! I'm the goddess of epic poetry! I've trained all of our previous bards! So, I _know_ I can coach you to speak in front of crowds! Whaddya say? Wanna travel to Mount Olympus with us?

JASON

You sure I'm the right guy?

CALLIOPE

As sure as Cerberus' three heads!

JASON

I don't know what that means… but, I do wanna see this mountain you're talking about.

CALLIOPE

That's good enough for me! Let's go!

Music #4b. Olympus – Part II

JASON

Are we gonna walk? Is it cold up there? What should I pack?

CALLIOPE

No time! We'll have to fly!

JASON

What?! You can fly?

HERMES

Of course we can, kid.

CALLIOPE

And Hermes here flies faster than any other god! We'll be on
Olympus in no time!

(JASON is so excited he can only utter nonsense.)

HERMES

Don't think your sweet talk changes my mind. If he's not
the next bard, this was all your fault!

*(CALLIOPE and HERMES take JASON'S hands and
fly off. The set transforms during the next sequence
into the grand halls of Mount Olympus, where
ATHENA, APHRODITE & ZEUS stand like mighty
statues, ready to welcome JASON. Among them is a
whole throng of GODS and MYTHICAL
CREATURES.)*

CALLIOPE

Here we go!
    OLYMPUS IS CALLING TO YOU
    OLYMPUS, WHERE STORIES COME TRUE
    OLYMPUS IS CALLING
    OLYMPUS, WE'RE FLYING AWAY
    TO OLYMPUS, THEN BACK THE SAME DAY
    OLYMPUS THE MOUNTAIN

HERMES, JASON

OLYMPUS THE MOUNTAIN

CALLIOPE

OLYMPUS THE MOUNTAIN

HERMES, JASON
OLYMPUS THE MOUNTAIN

CALLIOPE
OLYMPUS THE MOUNTAIN

ALL THREE
OF THE GODS!

CALLIOPE
Welcome to Mount Olympus, Jason!

JASON
Wow!

CALLIOPE
It's time to meet the other gods!

Music #4c. Olympus – Part III

CALLIOPE
First up, the Goddess of Beauty and Love: Aphrodite!

APHRODITE
Hello, handsome!

I'M APHRODITE
MY POWER'S MIGHTY
THE POWER OF LOVE
THE WORLD CAN'T GET ENOUGH
KEEP YOUR BRAINS AND YOUR BRAWN
MY HEART IS WHAT KEEPS ME STRONG

HERMES

And now, the goddess of wisdom and justice: Athena!

(ATHENA gives CALLIOPE a very displeased look.)

ATHENA

I refuse to recite this awful poetry.

CALLIOPE

Then we'll do it! Come on, Hermes!

(CALLIOPE and HERMES strike poses.)

ATHENA

Hera help us…

Music #4d. Olympus – Part IV

CALLIOPE

(rapping)
SHE IS ATHENA
THE BEST YOU'VE EVER SEEN-A

HERMES

BETTER WATCH, MANKIND
SHE'LL BEAT YOU WITH HER MIND

OTHER GODS

HUNH!

HERMES

SO INSTEAD OF JUMPING INTO A SORRY FIGHT

CALLIOPE

GONNA PLAY IT COOL!

HERMES

GONNA PLAY IT RIGHT!

CALLIOPE

ANYONE WHO TRIES TO MESS WITH HER IS
DONE

HERMES, CALLIOPE

'CAUSE SHE'S GOT THE POWER OF WIS-DOM

ATHENA

Is my part finished yet?

CALLIOPE

Going on! And now…

Music #4e. Olympus – Part V

CALLIOPE

The wielder of the thunderbolt!

HERMES

The strongest of all Olympians!

CALLIOPE

The king of the gods!

CALLIOPE, HERMES

Zeus!

ZEUS

(laughs powerfully)
BEHOLD ME!
YOU'RE LOOKIN' AT ZEUS!
BELIEVE ME
I'M HARD TO INTRODUCE
TOO MANY GREAT THINGS WOULD NEED TO BE
SAID
BUT I DON'T LET IT GET TO MY HEAD

ATHENA

Ha!

ZEUS

BEWARE OF
MY LIGHTNING BARRAGE!
BESIDE ME
MY ROYAL ENTOURAGE
READY TO MEET YOU AND GIVE YOU A SHOT
TO SHOW US ALL JUST WHAT YOU'VE GOT!
*(JASON faints into HERMES' arms. ZEUS is not
impressed.)*

ZEUS

Can we speed this along?

CALLIOPE

Certainly! Jason, meet the ENTIRE PANTHEON!

ALL EXCEPT JASON

OLYMPUS
YOU'VE FINALLY ARRIVED
AT OLYMPUS
WHERE MYTHS ARE ALIVE
OLYMPUS THE MOUNTAIN

JASON

OLYMPUS THE MOUNTAIN

ALL EXCEPT JASON

OLYMPUS THE MOUNTAIN

JASON

OLYMPUS THE MOUNTAIN

ALL EXCEPT JASON

OLYMPUS THE MOUNTAIN
OF THE GODS!

<u>**SCENE 2**</u>

CALLIOPE

Everyone, this is Jason, our new bard!

ZEUS

We are excited to have you here on Mount Olympus, mortal.
Gimme a fist bump!

JASON

You guys fist bump?

ZEUS

We've had several millennia to keep up with the times. In
fact, that's why you're here. Jason, everything today is "post
this" and "text that." But these aren't suitable ways for
keeping the tales of Olympus alive. Our stories were meant
to be narrated, performed, declared live before an audience!
So, I sent Calliope down to find someone who could
appreciate our stories and share them once again. And
apparently, that person is you. Now gimme a fist bump!

(They fist-bump.)

APHRODITE

Aw… our new bard is so adorable! Aren't you, new bard?

ATHENA

He's not our new bard yet.

CALLIOPE

Athena…

ATHENA

(to JASON)

I have a list of questions to ask you, Jason.

JASON

(getting very nervous)

Uh… OK.

CALLIOPE

This is so unnecessary!

ATHENA

I think we're entitled to a complete background check, Zeus.

CALLIOPE

Wait! Wait! I've seen Jason telling stories in his bedroom, and he's good! I'm talking like Homer good!

(The GODS strike a reverent pose at the mention of Homer.)

JASON

Who?

HERMES

Homer: our first bard.

CALLIOPE

Jason just doesn't know any of *our* stories because we aren't famous like we used to be! What if we started by sharing some of our favorite Greek myths with him?

ZEUS

Like a story sampler platter.

CALLIOPE

Exactly! Then, after some coaching from yours truly, we give him a chance to tell a tale of Olympus!

ATHENA
(sees ZEUS thinking about it)
Zeus, no…

ZEUS

Athena, stop being such a killjoy! Maybe Calliope's finally got it right this time!

HERMES

Good thinking, Zeus!

(CALLIOPE gives HERMES a look.)

APHRODITE

Olympus could do with some cheerful storytelling!

ZEUS

Mind if we put on a little show for you, mortal?

JASON

Are you kidding? That'd be awesome!

(ATHENA groans and walks away from the group.)

CALLIOPE

Jason, what kind of story do you wanna hear first?

JASON

I like stories that are epic! Like about a hero with a destiny!

ZEUS

Looks like it's time for my story.

JASON

Your story?

ZEUS

The tale of how Zeus became king of the gods!

CALLIOPE

Uh… Zeus, Jason's still getting to know us. Maybe we shouldn't go there.

ZEUS

Go where? To my own family history!?

CALLIOPE

Well, it's just that some of the details might be disturbing for a kid…

ZEUS

Nonsense! Jason can handle it! Besides, you wanted a hero story, right?

JASON

Sure!

ZEUS

So it's settled! Time for my story!

CALLIOPE

But –

ATHENA

(to CALLIOPE)

He's made up his mind. It's too late.

CALLIOPE

Sorry, Jason. Better brace yourself.

JASON

For what?

ZEUS

Jason, you should know that I come from a very messy family background.

ATHENA

That's a polite way of putting it.

ZEUS

It's so bad, it makes reality television look normal! Maestro?

Music #5a. The Baby Swallowing Song – Part I

(Various GODS from the ensemble step forward to act out ZEUS' words.)

ZEUS

LET'S GO BACK IN TIME
BEFORE HUMANKIND
JUST AFTER THE UNION OF EARTH AND SPACE
WHEN CRONUS WAS KING
AND RHEA WAS QUEEN
A MATCH MADE IN HEAVEN?
NO, THE OTHER PLACE!

ZEUS (CONT)
THE KING HAD RECENTLY BEEN TOLD
BY HIS FATHER, VERY, VERY OLD
THAT A CHILD OF HIS WOULD RISE TO STEAL
THE CROWN
CRONUS CRIED

CRONUS
"WHAT SHOULD I DO THEN, POP?"

ZEUS
HIS FATHER SAID "I KNOW A WAY TO STOP
THIS HORRIBLE PROPHECY!
JUST SWALLOW THOSE BABIES DOWN!"

JASON
What??

ZEUS
GULP! GULP! SWALLOW THOSE BABIES!
GULP! GULP! SWALLOW THOSE BABIES!
GULP! GULP! SWALLOW THOSE BABIES
DOWN FOR LUNCH!

ZEUS, CRONUS, GODS (EXCEPT ATHENA)
GULP! GULP! SWALLOW THOSE BABIES!
GULP! GULP! SWALLOW THOSE BABIES!
GULP! GULP! SWALLOW THOSE BABIES
DOWN FOR LUNCH!

JASON
That's horrible!

ZEUS

Are you interrupting me?!
> *(to the OTHER GODS)*
Did he just interrupt me?!

APHRODITE

It's OK, Jason. All of the babies in the story are immortal!

HERMES

That means they can't die.

APHRODITE

So, it's all going to turn out OK. Just listen.

Music #5b. The Baby Swallowing Song – Part II

ZEUS

THEN CRONUS RETURNED
WITH ALL THAT HE'D LEARNED
HE SAT DOWN FOR SUPPER WHEN RHEA SAID

RHEA

YOU'RE FINALLY A DAD

ZEUS

THEN CRONUS WENT MAD
THE SIGHT OF HIS KIDS FILLED HIS HEART
WITH DREAD
SO, KING CRONUS CARRIED OUT HIS PLAN
TO REINFORCE HIS RULING SPAN
HE WAITED TILL HIS WIFE WAS OUT OF TOWN
TRYING TO CHEAT HIS FUTURE FATE
HE PUT THOSE BABIES ON A PLATE
SHOUTED OUT

CRONUS
BOTTOMS UP!

ZEUS
AND SOON HE SWALLOWED THOSE BABIES
DOWN!

GULP! GULP! HE SWALLOWED THOSE BABIES!
GULP! GULP! SWALLOWED THOSE BABIES!
GULP! GULP! SWALLOWED THOSE BABIES!
DOWN ALIVE!

ALL GODS EXCEPT ATHENA
GULP! GULP! HE SWALLOWED THOSE BABIES!
GULP! GULP! SWALLOWED THOSE BABIES!
GULP! GULP!

ZEUS
MIRACULOUS THING THOUGH:
THEY SURVIVED!

RHEA
NOW RHEA PLAYED IT SMART
SHE KNEW HER HUSBAND'S WILES
SO SHE DECIDED TO FIGHT BACK
AND TOOK THE FINAL CHILD
REPLACED IT WITH A ROCK
HID BABY IN A CAVE

CRONUS
(eating the rock)
Nom, nom, nom!

RHEA
AND SOON THAT LITTLE BOY GREW UP
BIG AND BOLD AND BRAVE!

ZEUS
And can you guess who that child was?

SOON IT WAS TIME TO LEAVE THE NEST
AND MOTHER SENT ME ON A QUEST
BACK HOME TO SET MY SWALLOWED FAM'LY
FREE
SHE HANDED ME A SPECIAL BREW
GUARANTEED TO MAKE MY FATHER SPEW
HE THOUGHT HE WAS DRINKING UP HIS ROYAL
MORNING TEA!

One, two, three!

(CRONUS begins retching.)

ZEUS
OUT! OUT! OUT CAME THE BABIES!
OUT! OUT! OUT CAME THE BABIES!
OUT! OUT! OUT CAME THE BABIES
ONE BY ONE!

ALL GODS EXCEPT ATHENA
OUT! OUT! OUT CAME THE BABIES!
OUT! OUT! OUT CAME THE BABIES!
OUT! OUT! OUT CAME THE BABIES
FULLY GROWN!

*(As each GOD/GODDESS is introduced, they
appear.)*

ALL GODS EXCEPT ATHENA & ZEUS
HERA!

HERA
The goddess queen!

ALL GODS EXCEPT ATHENA & ZEUS
POSEIDON!

POSEIDON
The god of the sea!

ALL GODS EXCEPT ATHENA & ZEUS
DEMETER!

DEMETER
The goddess of harvest!

ALL GODS EXCEPT ATHENA & ZEUS
HESTIA!

HESTIA
The goddess of the flame!

ALL GODS EXCEPT ATHENA & ZEUS
AND HADES!

HADES
God of the Underworld.

ALL GODS EXCEPT ATHENA & ZEUS
Ooooo!

ZEUS

MY PROWESS NOW SHOWN
HAD DAD OVERTHROWN
HIS PARENTING HABITS WERE QUITE AMISS
OH YES, ONE MORE THING!
THAT'S HOW I BECAME KING!
BUT IF THERE'S ONE THING I LEARNED FROM
MY DAD
IT'S THIS
DON'T! DON'T SWALLOW A BABY!
DON'T! DON'T SWALLOW A BABY!
DON'T! DON'T SWALLOW A BABY!
IT IS WRONG!

Everybody!

ALL GODS EXCEPT ATHENA

DON'T! DON'T SWALLOW A BABY!
DON'T! DON'T SWALLOW A BABY!
DON'T! DON'T SWALLOW A BABY!
THAT IS WHY WE SING THIS SONG!

<u>SCENE 3</u>

ZEUS

A remarkable story, don't you think, mortal?

JASON

No, I don't! Anyone who enjoyed that story is sick in the head!

(ZEUS begins to charge angrily at JASON; HERMES and APHRODITE hold ZEUS back.)

CALLIOPE

Jason, there are some tales in our tradition that are... well, colorful.

JASON

Are all Greek myths this messed up?

HERMES

Pretty much.

(ATHENA begins laughing.)

ZEUS

What's so funny?

ATHENA

You. This.
> *(sighs)*

Unfortunately, Jason, you'll find that all of my colleagues have "colorful" histories.

ZEUS

Are you saying you're better than us?

ATHENA

I am, actually. When it comes to virtue and morality, I have
no equal.

CALLIOPE

Oh yeah, Athena? What about…

ALL GODS EXCEPT ATHENA

Arachne?

ATHENA

Don't you dare!

JASON

Who's Arachne?

ZEUS

A human who got on Athena's nerves. It all started –

ATHENA

Stop! You won't tell it right. Jason, it all started –
(stops herself, the addresses the other GODS)
I see what you're doing. You're trying to trick me into this
circus of storytelling!

ZEUS

Well, if you don't tell the story, I will –

ATHENA

Not on your best toga, you won't.

Music #6a. I Used to Weave – Part I

ATHENA

(relenting)
Jason, it all started because…

I USED TO WEAVE
TOYING WITH THREADS WAS A PASSION OF
MINE
I USED TO WEAVE
MIXING AND MATCHING AND MAKING DESIGNS
I USED TO SEW
PRETTY PATTERNS IN TAPESTRIES, COLORS
AGLOW
ONCE THE FAME OF MY ARTISTRY STARTED TO
GROW
THERE WAS NONE WHO COULD MIMIC ME, SO I
BELIEVED
I USED TO WEAVE
HOW I COULD WEAVE

OTHER GODS

WE DON'T MEAN TO DAMPEN YOUR GLORY
BUT PLEASE ADMIT
THIS IS NOT THE CORE OF YOUR STORY
GET ON WITH IT!

ATHENA

Allright! Along came Arachne. Another weaver. She was
small, pitiful, *mortal.* But she was also very, very good.

*(ARACHNE enters weaving while the others watch
on.)*

ARACHNE'S ADMIRERS
WATCH HOW SHE WEAVES!
SKILLFUL ARACHNE

ATHENA
I'M NOT THAT IMPRESSED

ARACHNE'S ADMIRERS
WATCH HOW SHE WEAVES!

ATHENA
FACE FULL OF ACNE
AND COMMONLY DRESSED!

ARACHNE
LOOK AT ME SEW

ARACHNE'S ADMIRERS
PRETTY PATTERNS AND TAPESTRIES

ARACHNE
COLORS AGLOW

ARACHNE'S ADMIRERS
DID YOU LEARN FROM ATHENA?

ARACHNE
ATHENA? GODS, NO!
BUT ATHENA COULD LEARN A FEW POINTERS
FROM ME!

ATHENA

That's it!
WHO DO YOU THINK YOU ARE, YOU SORRY
LITTLE AMATEUR?
YOU THINK YOU'RE BETTER THAN A GODDESS,
HONEY?
YEAH, I'M SURE!
LET'S PUT YOUR QUESTIONABLE THEORY TO
THE TEST

ARACHNE

I'M IN!

ATHENA

WE'LL HAVE A TOURNAMENT
AND SHE WHO WEAVES THE BEST WILL WIN!

AN ADMIRER

Ready, set, go!

ARACHNE'S ADMIRERS

LOOK AT THEM WEAVE
THEIR HANDS ARE FLYING, THEIR FACES ARE
TENSE
LOOK AT THEM WEAVE
THREADING AND TYING, SUCH KNOTTED
SUSPENSE!

ATHENA

OH, HOW I BLAZED
HOW I WANTED THE WORSHIP, THE POMP AND
THE PRAISE!
I COULD SWEAR I WAS WEAVING AND WEAVING
FOR DAYS

ATHENA (CONT)
THEN WE FINALLY STOPPED AND THE WEAVING
WAS DONE!

*(ATHENA and ARACHNE both hold up their
finished tapestries.)*

ATHENA
And not only was her design good – it was better than mine.

Music #6c. I Used to Weave – Part III

ATHENA
BUT I HAD TOO MUCH PRIDE IN MY HEART
TO ADMIT SHE HAD WON!

SO I DID WHAT ANY GODDESS WOULD DO
I KNEW JUST HOW TO PUNISH AND SMITE HER!
SO SHE WANTED TO WEAVE?
WELL, ALLRIGHT THEN, SHE'D WEAVE!
ALL HER DAYS AS AN EIGHT-LEGGED SPIDER!

(ARACHNE screams and becomes a spider.)

ARACHNE'S ADMIRERS
(walking away)
So not cool, Athena…, Show off…, etc.

ATHENA
Wait, come back! Now I'm the master weaver! Don't you
want to see my tapestry?

(ATHENA turns slowly and sadly toward JASON.)

ATHENA

LISTEN, MY BOY
I JUST HAD TO BE BEST, SO THE BEST I
DESTROYED
NOW I'M BEST OF WHO'S LEFT, BUT I'VE LOST
ALL THE JOY
OF CREATING A BLANKET, A SCARF OR A
SLEEVE
AND EACH SPIDER I SEE IS A REASON TO
GRIEVE
I USED TO WEAVE
I USED TO WEAVE

OTHER GODS

DON'T BE SAD, ATHENA
WE ALL LOSE OUR COOL SOMETIMES
YOU'RE NOT BAD, ATHENA
WE ALL ACT THE FOOL SOMETIMES

SCENE 4

JASON

Athena… I really liked your story. It was a little bit sad, but in a good way. And it made me think about times when I should have been nicer to people. So, thank you.

ATHENA
(starting to be impressed by JASON)
Jason. You possess a wisdom beyond your years.

JASON

I guess there can be something to learn from any story, no matter how messed up the characters are.

ATHENA
(a bit offended)
Thank you…

CALLIOPE

So you like our stories?

JASON

Yes. There are some good lessons people could learn from them. Don't get jealous of others. Don't swallow babies…

CALLIOPE
(giddily hugs JASON, then to the OTHERS)
See? Only a true storyteller could understand all that so fast! The soul of a bard.

ZEUS

Does this mean you're ready to perform for us now?

JASON
(nervous at the thought of having to perform)
Huh? Uh… no. I need to hear a few more stories first.

CALLIOPE
But why?

JASON
Why? Well… Because I -
(finding an excuse)
I'm not convinced yet that this is a good fit.

APHRODITE
But you just said you liked our stories.

JASON
I do… It's just that…
(gets a thought)
Kids!

ZEUS
What?

JASON
You can't just have stories about *adult* gods and goddesses. There needs to be a story about a kid… for us kids to relate to…

CALLIOPE
The story of Icarus! He wasn't a god, but he was a kid.

ATHENA
And Icarus was around your age when this story takes place.

JASON

(falsely reassuring)
Yes, that's perfect. I'll be able to relate to him.

ZEUS

Why don't we have the Muses narrate this one? Calliope?

CALLIOPE

Only if Athena joins too!

JASON

Please, Athena? I'd love to see you perform again.

ATHENA

Why not? I'll play King Minos!

ZEUS

(gloating)
I knew you'd come around.

Music #7. Icarus and Daedalus

HERMES

(to JASON)
You'll like this one, kid! It's a story about *flying!*

CLIO

DAEDALUS WAS A SKILLFUL MAN
KNOWN FOR BUILDING WITH HIS HANDS
MADE A LABYRINTH MASTER PLAN
FOR A KING CALLED MINOS

URANIA, THALIA
ICARUS WAS A FOOLISH SON
ALWAYS SOUGHT TO HAVE SOME FUN
LOVED TO PLAY AND JUMP AND RUN
NEVER ONE FOR SHYNESS

ICARUS
(playing with DAEDALUS' work tools)
Hey Dad, look at me! I'm the Gorgon, Medusa!

DAEDALUS
Son, I'm trying to work!

MUSES
THE LAB'RINTH WAS INTENDED FOR
A MINOTAUR, THEY SAY
WITH THE HEAD OF A BULL AND THE BODY OF
A MAN AND –

ATHENA
WELL, THAT'S A STORY FOR ANOTHER DAY

MUSES
WORKING, WORKING
DAEDALUS WORKING OH SO HARD!
WORKING, WORKING
DAEDALUS WORKING HARD!
PLAYING, PLAYING
ICARUS PLAYING OH SO HARD!
PLAYING, PLAYING
ICARUS PLAYING HARD!

TERPSICHORE, ERATO
NOW, WHEN THE LABYRINTH WAS DONE
KING MINOS, HE WAS CALLOUS
HE SHOUTED

ATHENA (MINOS)
"I DON'T TRUST YOU, SON!'"

TERPSICHORE, ERATO
AND LOCKED THEM IN HIS PALACE

ATHENA (MINOS)
"If I don't lock him up, then he'll tell everyone the solution
to my labyrinth! Then my mighty Minotaur will never get to
eat people. And where's the fun in that?"
(lets out a crazy laugh)

MUSES
IN A HIGH, HIGH TOWER IN HIS PALACE!
LOCKED UP, LOCKED UP
BOTH OF 'EM LOCKED UP IN A TOWER
LOCKED UP, LOCKED UP
LOCKED UP IN A TOWER

POLYHYMNIA
DAEDALUS DID NOT GIVE UP HOPE
THOUGH HE'D REACHED THE END OF ROPE
WORKING HARD WAS HOW HE'D COPE
HOUR BY THE HOUR

EUTERPE, MELPOMENE
ICARUS WAS A RESTLESS SOUL
BEING LOCKED UP TOOK ITS TOLL
STARTED FEELING LIKE A MOLE
COOPED UP IN THE TOWER

ICARUS

Dad, I need to get out of here!

DAEDALUS

All right, son!

> *(DAEDALUS holds two pairs of wings and hands
> one pair to ICARUS.)*

DAEDALUS

HERE'S A PAIR OF WAXEN WINGS
COME ON AND HAVE A TRY
WE'LL STAND ON THE LEDGE OF THE WINDOW
AND THEN
WE'LL JUMP AND FLAP AND FLY!

ICARUS

Wicked awesome cool!!!

DAEDALUS

Now, Icarus, before we take off, heed my words.

DON'T FLY TOO HIGH TO THE SUN, OR ELSE
THE WINGS WILL MELT AWAY
DON'T FLY TOO LOW TO OCEAN, OR ELSE
YOU'LL BE SUCKED IN BY THE SPRAY
NOW REPEAT AFTER ME:

DON'T FLY TOO HIGH

ICARUS

DON'T FLY TOO HIGH

DAEDALUS

DON'T FLY TOO LOW

ICARUS

DON'T FLY TOO LOW

DAEDALUS

GOT IT?

ICARUS

GOT IT.

DAEDALUS

NOW I'LL JUMP FIRST, YOU LEARN FROM ME
AND WATCH ME GO!

ICARUS, MUSES

FLYING FLYING
DAEDALUS FLYING IN THE SKY
FLYING FLYING
DAEDALUS FLYING HIGH!

FLY, DAEDALUS, FLY!
FLY! FLY! FLY!
FLY, DAEDALUS, FLY!
FLY! FLY! FLY!

DAEDALUS

Now follow me, son!

ICARUS

Here I come!

DAEDALUS, MUSES

FLYING, FLYING
ICARUS FLYING IN THE SKY
FLYING, FLYING
ICARUS FLYING HIGH!

ICARUS*

Hey, look at me!
I'M FLYING, FLYING
LOOK AT ME FLYING IN THE SKY
FLYING, FLYING
LOOK AT ME FLYING HIGH!

DAEDALUS, MUSES*
(simultaneously with HERMES)

FLY, ICARUS, FLY! FLY! FLY! FLY!
FLY, ICARUS, FLY! FLY! FLY! FLY!

DAEDALUS

Don't fly too high!

ICARUS

What was that? Fly even *higher!?*

MUSES

FLYING, FLYING
ICARUS FLYING IN THE SKY!
FLYING, FLYING
ICARUS FLYING HIGHER
AND HIGHER AND HIGHER AND HIGHER AND
HIGHER

ICARUS

Phew! It's hot up here! Uh oh… My wings!

MUSES
MELTING, MELTING
WINGS ARE MELTING FROM THE HEAT
MELTING, MELTING

GASP!

FLAPPING, FLAPPING
ICARUS FLAPPING FRANTIC'LY!
FLAPPING, FLAPPING
FLAPPING FRANTIC'LY!

NO USE!
FALLING, FALLING
ICARUS FALLING FROM THE SKY
FALLING, FALLING
FALLING, FALLING
FALLING, FALLING

SPLASH!

GODS
HERE'S THE LESSON, EVERYONE
EVERY DAUGHTER, EVERY SON
IF YOU'RE PRONE TO HAVING FUN
ONE THING IS APPARENT

YES, IT MUST BE UNDERSTOOD
FOR YOUR SAFETY, FOR YOUR GOOD
YOU'LL BE WISER IF YOU WOULD
LISTEN TO YOUR PARENTS!

LISTEN, LISTEN
LISTEN TO YOUR PARENTS, KIDS!

GODS (CONT)

LISTEN, LISTEN
TO YOUR PARENTS, KIDS!

LISTEN, LISTEN
LISTEN TO YOUR PARENTS, KIDS!
LISTEN, LISTEN
DON'T END UP LIKE ICARUS DID!

SCENE 5

CALLIOPE

Was that a good kid story?

JASON

There's still a tragic ending for Icarus, but it comes with a very important lesson. So yes, that was a very good kid story. Tell me another one!

ZEUS

Nope. Time for *you* to tell *us* a story, storyteller!

JASON

Really? Does it have to be now?

APHRODITE

There's no better time!

CALLIOPE

Especially if you're going to be our next bard!

JASON

But I can't – I can't do the job… People… Crowds…

(Understanding the situation, JASON almost faints again.)

ZEUS

What's his problem?

HERMES

He has a fear of public speaking.

ALL OTHER GODS

What!?

ZEUS

(to HERMES)
You waited until now to tell us?

CALLIOPE

I know it looks bad…

ZEUS

Hephaestus! Get me my new thunderbolts!

ATHENA

Zeus, calm down.

ZEUS

How can you expect me to –

ATHENA

We need to find a rational solution.

ZEUS

And what do you propose?

CALLIOPE

Jason can be trained.

ZEUS

(to HERMES)
You knew about this the whole time, didn't you?

CALLIOPE

If you would just listen to me…

(Arguments among the GODS escalates.)

(APHRODITE uses her power of love to bring calm. As she sings, the OTHERS stop their squabbling.)

APHRODITE

OOOH…
OOOH…

JASON

What just happened?

HERMES

Aphrodite's song. It turns people's hearts towards love.

APHRODITE

And this mountain needs a lotta love right now. Yes, we're short on time. But instead of fighting about it, let's give Jason a chance. We've seen how much he loves stories! And Calliope told us he has the soul of a bard. And if the goddess of epic poetry says Jason can be trained, well I'm going to believe her.

ATHENA

I never thought I'd say this, but your point is sound, Aphrodite.

APHRODITE

Zeus?

ZEUS

He's afraid of speaking in public.

APHRODITE

Yes, it seems like quite the conundrum. But even in the worst situations, there's always hope! Remember Pandora?

CALLIOPE

Pandora, yes! That's a nice, simple story to start Jason off with.

JASON

Excuse me?

CALLIOPE

(to JASON)
Practice starts now! And we'll help you!

ZEUS

Excuse *me?*

CALLIOPE

He needs some training and time is ticking! What do you say? Let's all help him tell this story.

APHRODITE

As long as Jason is willing.

JASON

(looks at CALLIOPE, then turns to the OTHERS)
I can try…

APHRODITE

Good. I'll narrate the story and play Pandora. Jason, you and the others can be Pandora's conscience.

CALLIOPE

(hands JASON a page)

Here – there are only five words you need to know to tell this story.

JASON

"Don't open the box, Pandora."

APHRODITE

You got it, cutie.

(Everyone gets into place. There is some bustling as JASON is not sure where he is supposed to stand.)

APHRODITE

Pandora was the first woman created by the gods. Upon her birth, the gods gave her the gift of a box, which she was never supposed to open under any circumstances.

JASON

How is that a gift?

(ZEUS gives JASON a stare.)

APHRODITE

At first, Pandora's conscience seemed in good order.

Music #9a. Don't Open the Box – Part I

HERMES & BASS
WE SAID DON'T, DON'T, DON'T

*(Parts marked with a * are sung simultaneously.)*

JASON & MELODY*

DON'T OPEN THE BOX, PANDORA
DON'T OPEN THE BOX, PANDORA
DON'T OPEN THE BOX
DON'T OPEN THE BOX
DON'T OPEN THE BOX!

ZEUS & TENORS*

DON'T OPEN THE BOX, PANDORA
NO, YOU DON'T!
OPEN THE BOX, PANDORA
DON'T OPEN THE BOX
DON'T OPEN THE BOX
DON'T OPEN THE BOX!

HERMES & BASSES*

DON'T, DON'T, DON'T, DON'T
DON'T, DON'T, DON'T, DON'T
DON'T OPEN THE BOX!
DON'T, DON'T, DON'T
DON'T OPEN THE BOX

APHRODITE

But as time wore on, she found the voices started to turn
sinister.

JASON, OTHER GODS

(They turn on PANDORA in sinister voices.)
OPEN THE BOX! OPEN THE BOX! OPEN IT!

(They return back to their cheerful song.)

JASON/CALLIOPE/MELODY*
OH NO!
NO!
DON'T OPEN THE BOX
DON'T OPEN THE BOX

ZEUS/TENORS & ATHENA/ALTOS*
DON'T OPEN THE BOX, PANDORA
DON'T EVEN TRY OR YOU'RE GOING TO
REGRET IT, DON'T!
DON'T OPEN THE BOX
DON'T OPEN THE BOX

HERMES/BASSES*
WE SAID DON'T, DON'T, DON'T, DON'T
WE SAID DON'T, DON'T, DON'T
DON'T, DON'T, DON'T, DON'T

JASON, OTHER GODS
(suddenly sinister again)
OPEN THE BOX! OPEN IT!

HERMES/BASSES
(disagreeing with the rest of her conscience)
DON'T!

JASON & ALL OTHER GODS
(insisting)
OPEN THE BOX! OPEN THE BOX! OPEN IT!

HERMES/BASSES

DON'T!
    (seeing the stares of the others, they relent)
ALLRIGHT, FINE!
OPEN THE BOX, OPEN THE BOX, OPEN IT!

HERMES/BASSES, ZEUS/TENORS, JASON/
CALLIOPE/MELODY

OPEN THE BOX, OPEN THE BOX, OPEN IT!

ALL GODS EXCEPT APHRODITE

OPEN THE BOX, OPEN THE BOX, OPEN IT! AAH!!!

APHRODITE (PANDORA)

I can't stand it!

Music #9c. Don't Open the Box – Part III

    (PANDORA opens the box and the OTHER GODS
    portray all of the evils of the world flying out.
    JASON follows along as best as he can.)

APHRODITE

As soon as she opened the box, all the evils of the world
sprang forth!

DESTRUCTION

Death and destruction!

DISEASE

Disease and decay!

JASON

Homework and going to the dentist!

JASON

Hey, I'm making it up as I go!

APHRODITE

Pandora thought she was utterly ruined. But suddenly, out from the box sprang… Hope!

Music #10. Hope's Solo

HOPE

FEAR NOT, PANDORA
FOR YOU'VE SET ME FREE
SURE YOU ALSO SET THOSE EVILS FREE

But, let's not dwell on the past…

THOUGH I MAY LOOK WEAK AND POCKET-
SIZED
YOU CAN BET I'LL SEE YOU THROUGH
FOR WHEREVER EVIL WAGES WAR
THERE I'LL BE FIGHTING TOO

APHRODITE

And so, even in the midst of darkness, Hope entered the world. And we cannot give up hope now.

CALLIOPE

Jason! You told your first tale of Olympus!

HERMES

Yeah, you did good, kid!

ZEUS

He was acceptable.

HERMES

(changing his mind)
You were acceptable, kid.

ATHENA

I agree. I think he needs to narrate a more elaborate tale.

JASON

More? But I don't know what story to tell.

CALLIOPE

What about the myth you're named after? The myth of the Greek hero Jason!

JASON

Hero? *I'm* named after a *hero?!*

HERMES

Jason and his mighty band of warriors, the Argonauts!

JASON
(excitedly begins battling imaginary foes)
He has warriors too?

CALLIOPE
I think he's interested…

HERMES
You won't know till you try!

APHRODITE
And we'll all help you tell it.
(to ZEUS and ATHENA)
Right?

ATHENA
It is the reasonable thing to do.

(They look to ZEUS.)

ZEUS
If the mortal is up for the challenge…

(The GODS all stare at JASON as he thinks.)

JASON
Let's do it!

(They cheer and encourage him.)

ZEUS
(laughing his deep laugh)

That's the spirit, Jason. OK, Olympians! This is a big one! More characters! More props! But, let's take no more than fifteen minutes maximus to get ready!

Music #11. Olympus (Reprise)

GODS

OLYMPUS IS GETTING PREPARED
OLYMPUS

> *(The GODS get ready for the tale of JASON. Possibly exiting the stage for costume shift if necessary.)*

JASON

I'M STILL FEELING SCARED
BUT I ALSO FEEL STRONG NOW
WITH GODS ON MY SIDE
AND IF IT GOES WRONG NOW
AT LEAST I HAD TRIED
IF I'M REALLY THEIR BARD
WHY AM I SO PETRIFIED?

<u>**SCENE 7**</u>

(HERMES walks across the stage with a sign that reads "NO MORE THAN FIFTEEN MINUTES MAXIMUS LATER." CALLIOPE hands JASON the book to read from, then leaves him alone on-stage.)

JASON
(nervously)
The Myth of the Greek Hero Jason.

Music #12a. Be A Hero – Part I

(AESON, PELIAS and ALCIMEDE enter as JASON narrates.)

JASON
Aeson was king of Thessaly. He had a brother named Pelias, a wife named Alcimede and a son named Jason – I'll be playing Jason, shortly.

Music #12b. Be A Hero – Part II

JASON
Pelias was jealous of his brother, so he overthrew Aeson and made himself king.

PELIAS
I overthrow you brother, and make myself king!

AESON
Nooo!

(AESON exits.)

JASON

Not long after this, an oracle came to Pelias.

ORACLE

(mysteriously)
I am the oracle. I see all that is to come.

PELIAS

And what is to come?

ORACLE

Beware the man with only one handle.

(Music stops abruptly.)

PELIAS

One handle? What does that mean?

ORACLE

Oops. I'm sorry. I meant one *sandal*. Sometimes my
reception cuts in and out. I gotta change providers.
(suddenly back to being mysterious)
Beware the man with only one sandal!

*(JASON is getting more comfortable and refers to
his script less and less, eventually doing away with it
altogether.*

JASON

Now, Alcimede knew that her son Jason was in danger because of uncle Pelias. So she gave him to Chiron – a centaur. Half man and half horse.

(CHIRON enters.)

ALCIMEDE

(sobbing uncontrollably)
Please take care of my child and raise him as your own.

CHIRON

I swear by the *neigh*-me of Zeus!

ALCIMEDE

Thank you, Chiron!

(CHIRON whinnies.)

Music #12e. Be A Hero – Part V

JASON

Jason grew up under Chiron's care. And one day:

CHIRON

Jason, it's time for you to return to your kingdom, overthrow your uncle and become the rightful king of Thessaly!

JASON

Do you really think I have what it takes?

CHIRON

Yes, my boy! And not only that! You will save us all from Pelias' horrible rule!

YOU WILL BE A HERO!
IF YOU TAKE YOUR PLACE ON THE THRONE
YOU'LL BE A HERO!
THERE'S A PROPHECY SET IN STONE
THAT A MAN WILL APPEAR
AND KICK PELIAS OUT
AND THEN EV'RYONE HERE
WILL HOLLER AND SHOUT
FOR OUR HERO,
SO YOU BETTER NOT POSTPONE!

Now get out there Jason, and termi-*neigh*-te your Uncle's reign!

(CHIRON exits. HERA enters disguised as an OLD WOMAN.)

JASON

So Jason set off to Pallis' paylice. Paylis' peelice.

OTHERS

Pelias' Palace!

JASON

Right. There. But on the way, he met an old woman trying to cross a river.

OLD WOMAN (HERA)

Would you help me, kind sir, to cross this river?

JASON

Sure, old woman!

(JASON carries her across the river.)

JASON

As Jason was crossing, he lost one of his sandals.

Music #12f. Be A Hero – Part VI

(ORACLE enters suddenly.)

ORACLE

Beware the man with only one sandal!

(ORACLE exits suddenly.)

JASON

Here you go!

OLD WOMAN (HERA)

Thank you, kind sir. Now I will reveal myself to you!

Music #12g. Be A Hero – PART VII

JASON

And she turned out to be Hera, the Goddess Queen!

HERA

I JUST WANTED TO TEST YOU
SEE HOW KIND YOU WOULD BE
AND YOU ARE! SO I BLESS YOU
NOW YOU'RE SPONSORED BY ME!
GO BE A HERO!

HERA (CONT)
AND I'LL BE YOUR BIGGEST FAN!

(HERA exits. PELIAS re-enters.)

JASON

Finally, Jason arrived at Palias' Pellas…

OTHERS

Pelias' Palace!

JASON

I, Jason, have arrived to take the throne as the rightful king of Thessaly!

PELIAS

Jason! Nephew! You've grown so tall! Give your old uncle a hug!

(PELIAS sees the missing sandal.)

Music #12h. Be A Hero – Part VIII

PELIAS

It can't be!

(ORACLE enters suddenly.)

ORACLE

Beware the man with only one –

PELIAS

Ok! I get it!

(ORACLE whimpers off.)

PELIAS

(to himself)
I NEED TO GET RID OF JASON
GET HIM OUT OF MY HAIR
I KNOW! I'LL SEND HIM OUT TRAV'LING
AND I KNOW JUST WHERE!
(speaks to JASON)
Of course, Jason, you can have the throne. But only if you bring back… THE GOLDEN FLEECE!

GODS

THE GOLDEN FLEECE!

PELIAS

Yes! The golden fleece guarded by the dragon that never sleeps!

GODS

THE GOLDEN FLEECE
GUARDED BY THE DRAGON
THAT NEVER SLEEPS!

JASON

That sounds hard.

PELIAS

It is. But if you accomplish it, Jason, do you know what that would make you?

JASON

I can guess.

PELIAS
OH, YOU WILL BE A HERO!
SO GO GET THAT GOLDEN FLEECE!
OH YEAH!

GODS
GO GET THAT GOLDEN FLEECE!
GO GET THAT GOLDEN FLEECE!

*(PELIAS exits. HERACLES and ATALANTA join
JASON on the Argo as they are announced.)*

JASON
So, Jason soon assembled a team of warriors including:

GODS
HERACLES!

HERACLES
I'M SO STRONG!

GODS
AND ATALANTA!

ATALANTA
I FIGHT LIKE A LION! ROWR!

JASON
Then they boarded the sturdy ship called The Argo! Ergo,
they became known as the Argonauts!
*(As the hero JASON, he speaks to HERACLES and
ATALANTA)*

JASON (CONT)

Let's ship out, warriors!

Music #12j. Be A Hero – Part X

HERACLES, ATALANTA

YOU'RE GONNA BE A HERO!

JASON

WITH MY FAITHFUL FRIENDS AND BOAT!

HERACLES, ATALANTA

GO, ARGO, GO, GO ARGO!
A HERO!

JASON

LET ME AT THAT DRAGON'S THROAT!
BUT THE JOURNEY WAS ROUGH
WE MET DANGEROUS FOES

HERACLES

LIKE THE SIX-ARMED GIANTS!

(SIX-ARMED GIANT appears.)

ATALANTA

AND THE HARPIES!

(HARPIES appear.)

JASON

What are those?

ATALANTA

Hungry bird-women who want to eat everything in sight!

JASON

Sounds like my Aunt Sophie!

HERMES

Hey, he made a joke!

(They all congratulate him.)

JASON

And… the story!

Music #12k. Be A Hero – Part XI

JASON

(as the hero)
Back off, Giant! Back off, Harpies!

(JASON, HERACLES & ATALANTA wrestle them away.)

JASON

Finally, they arrived at the Kingdom of Colchis where the Golden Fleece was kept.

GODS

THE GOLDEN FLEECE!

JASON

The king of Colchis was Aetes. And Aetes had a daughter named Medea.

(AETES enters – he should be played by the same actor as PELIAS. MEDEA also enters.)

66

GODS

(a la opera)

AH!

MEDEA

I'M A MAGICAL WOMAN
A SORC'RESS THEY SAY

ZEUS

BUT THIS SHOW'S NOT ABOUT YOU
THAT'S A WHOLE 'NOTHER PLAY!

MEDEA

Several plays, actually. And some operas, some films, some
books –

AETES

(interrupting her)
Medea! We have a visitor!
(to JASON)
I am King Aeeeetes! What can I do for you?

JASON

King Aeeeetes!

Music #12l. Be A Hero – Part XII

JASON

I have come to get the Golden Fleece guarded by the Dragon
That Never Sleeps!

GODS

THE GOLDEN FLEECE
GUARDED BY THE DRAGON
THAT NEVER SLEEPS!

AETES
(falls to the floor with overwhelmed laughter)

I'm sorry. I thought you said you wanted to get the Golden
Fleece guarded by the Dragon That Never Sleeps!

GODS

THE GOLDEN –

AETES

Ok! We get it!

JASON

That's what I said!

AETES

Good luck with that.
(to MEDEA)
He'll soon be dead.

HERA

Not if I have anything to do about it! Get to it, girl!

*(HERA pushes APHRODITE out to the center like a
sports coach.)*

Music #12m. Be A Hero – Part XIII

APHRODITE

Right!

I'M APHRODITE!
MY POWER'S MIGHTY
MY POWER, NO DOUBT,
WILL HELP BRAVE JASON OUT.
OOH

JASON

And she cast a spell upon Medea, making her fall in love
with Jason.

MEDEA

Hubba hubba! A-oo-ga! A-oo-ga!

*(pants like a dog, or any other cartoon-y way of
showing she's in love)*

APHRODITE

My work here is done.

MEDEA

I'll help you get that fleece, Jason.

JASON

You will?

MEDEA

Sure. And I'll even show you where that mean, old dragon
sleeps!

JASON

Thanks, Medea.
>   *(to HERACLES & ATALANTA)*
I have to do this alone, warriors.

>   *(HERACLES and ATALANTA grumble as they exit.)*

JASON

>   *(to MEDEA)*
Take me to him!

Music #12n. Be A Hero – Part XIV

GODS

AH!

>   *(Several GODS enter as the DRAGON.)*

DRAGON

I AM
THE DRAGON
THAT NEVER SLEEPS!
>   *(Repeats underneath dialogue.)*

JASON

Such a beast! But no match for my sword.

>   *(He pulls out a tiny sword.)*

MEDEA

Uh… Jason, I dunno about that…

JASON

Consider this dragon a goner!

70

(He moves to attack, but MEDEA blocks him.)

MEDEA

Wait! What if I just used my dragon-slumber potion?

JASON

That sounds good.

(MEDEA sprinkles the potion on the dragon.)

DRAGON

I AM
THE DRAGON
THAT NEVER SLEEPS
AND BOY, AM I TIRED…
    (DRAGON yawns)
Thank you…

(The DRAGON falls asleep.)

MEDEA

Jason! The fleece!

Music #12o. Be A Hero – Part XV

(JASON grabs the fleece and holds it up victoriously. HERMES re-enters as AETES.)

GODS

THE GOLDEN FLEECE!

AETES

Impossible!

MEDEA

Goodbye, Father.

AETES

Goodbye?!

MEDEA

I'm going back with Jason, my love!

AETES

I forbid it!

> *(MEDEA pulls out another potion and sprinkles it on the DRAGON. The DRAGON chases KING AETES off.)*

Music #12p. Be A Hero – Part XVI

AETES

AEEEEEEEEE!!!!

MEDEA

My special dragon-awakening-and-father-chasing potion.

JASON

Come on, Medea. I've got a kingdom to claim!

Music #12q. Be A Hero – Part XVII

JASON, GODS
WE'RE JOURNEYING BACK TO THE KINGDOM
WE'RE JOURNEYING BACK TO THE KINGDOM

> *(PELIAS re-enters.)*

PELIAS

Jason?! Impossible!

JASON

Goodbye, Uncle!

PELIAS

Goodbye?!

JASON

I have it! I have the Golden Fleece! The throne is mine!

PELIAS

AEEEEEEEEEE!!!

(PELIAS runs off.)

Music #12r. Be A Hero – Part XVIII

MEDEA

Jason! You did it!

JASON

I did it!

GODS

He did it!
NOW YOU ARE A HERO!
AFTER TRAVELING FAR AND WIDE

JASON

YEAH, YEAH, YEAH, YEAH!

GODS

NOW YOU ARE A HERO!

JASON

WITH THIS TWENTY-FOUR KARAT HIDE!

GODS

HIDE!

JASON

I AM VALIANT AND BRAVE
I'M COURAGEOUS AND BOLD
I AM FEARLESS AND NOBLE
MAY IT ALWAYS BE TOLD
HOW I'M DAUNTLESS AND DARING
I'VE GOT GRIT! I'VE GOT GUTS!
IF THEY TRY TO DEFEAT ME
WELL, THEY'VE GOT TO BE NUTS!

CAUSE I AM A HERO!

GODS

OH YES, HE IS A HERO

JASON

I AM A HERO!

GODS

OH YES, HE IS A HERO

JASON

A HERO!

GODS

OH YES, HE IS A HERO
YES, YES, YES, YES!

ALL

JASON IS A HERO!

75

<u>**SCENE 8**</u>

(THE GODS all congratulate JASON. CALLIOPE motions that a ceremony is beginning.)

Music #13a. Finale – Part I

CALLIOPE
I, Calliope, Goddess of Epic Poetry officially dub you, Jason, the new bard of the Greek gods!

Music #13b. Finale – Part II

(The OTHERS cheer as CALLIOPE hands JASON a lyre.)

GODS
HE'LL TELL OUR STORIES!
HE'LL TELL OUR STORIES!

(They stand around JASON.)

CALLIOPE
Jason, I'm afraid it's time for you to return home.

APHRODITE
But we'll see you soon for rehearsals, you adorable, little bard, you.

JASON
We'll practice here on Olympus, right?

ZEUS
There's no better place, is there?

(ZEUS and JASON do another fist bump.)

ATHENA
Are you ready to go home, Jason?

JASON
(gives it some thought, then confidently responds)
Yes. Goodbye, everyone!

GODS
Goodbye! Bye, Jason! Etc.

Music #13c. Finale – Part III

(JASON is transported back into his bedroom. He looks around the room in wonder.)

JASON
WAS I REALLY ON THAT MOUNTAIN?
(sees he is still holding the lyre)
YES! HERE'S THE PROOF THAT I WAS
SCHMOOZING WITH THE GODS!
NOW THEY'VE GIVEN ME A JOB TO DO
AND I PROMISED THEM I'D FOLLOW THROUGH
SO GET READY WORLD FOR THE BIG DEBUT
OF YOUR LATEST, GREATEST BARD!

CAUSE I HAVE A STORY
EVERY SINGLE SENTENCE, EVERY WORD
QUITE THE STORY
SO, LET IT BE HEARD!

I'M FINALLY VENTURING OUT OF MY SHELL

JASON (CONT)

AT FIRST I WAS NERVOUS, BUT NOW I FEEL
SWELL
I'LL JUMP, SING AND SHOUT, AND I'LL DANCE
AND I'LL YELL!
CAUSE I HAVE A STORY
TO TELL!

GODS

I HAVE A STORY

JASON

TO TELL!

GODS

I HAVE A STORY
OOO…

JASON

(declaring it to the world)
My name's Jason. And I am a storyteller!

GODS

AH!

(Blackout.)

Music #14. Bows

(End of play.)

* 9 7 8 1 9 6 8 0 5 1 4 9 5 *